D0556687

Country Pleasures
by John Gill

For FERNANDO—
with thanks for a
very fine "working"
visit.

John Gill
4/4/81

Introduction by Victor Contoski
Illustrations by Harley Elliott

The Crossing Press // Trumansburg, N.Y.

ACKNOWLEDGMENTS

Books: *Young Man's Letter*, 1967, New/Books (The
         Crossing Press).
         Gill's Blues, 1969, New/Books (The Crossing Press).

Edited: *New American and Canadian Poetry*, 1971,
         Beacon Press.

Magazine publications:
         *Aldebaran Review, Dacotah Territory, December,
         Four Elements, Granite, Greenfield Review,
         Hanging Loose, Hearse, La Huerta, Minnesota
         Review, Northeast, TCB, Three Rivers Poetry
         Journal, Poetry Now, Valley Magazine.*

Scolnik Sykes Design
Photograph by James Jackson

This project is supported by a grant from the National
Endowment for the Arts in Washington, D.C., a Federal
agency.

THE CROSSING PRESS SERIES OF SELECTED POETS

Second Printing, 1977

Library of Congress Cataloging in Publication Data

Gill, John, 1924-
   Country Pleasures.

   (The Crossing Press series of selected poets)
   I. Title.
PS3557.I369C6   811'.5'2   75-28398
ISBN 0-912278-60-9
ISBN 0-912278-61-7 pbk.
ISBN 0-912278-70-6 lim. ed.

Dedicated to Elaine

Contents

Introduction

Country Pleasures, as its title suggests, is frankly hedonistic, applying the most appealing elements of the pastoral tradition--its return to nature, its melancholy, its sensuality, and its tendency toward moralization--to American life in the twentieth century.

But Gill's pastoralism is above all realistic. The short first section leads us from life in Chicago to a proclamation of another kind of life in "Manifesto," a life which we see in the second section as the poet takes us to Trumansburg, New York. It begins uneasily. In "Something More Ghostly" we camp on conquered ground. . .

> and something more ghostly rings us in
> a restlessness, a vague fear, a distaste
> as simple as the weather
> for this quietly spectacular land. . .

Once into the countryside we discover the violence hidden from city-dwellers. A slaughtered steer lies on the ground, legs up, decapitated. Men come "stripping   gutting   sawing." Owls hunt their "purses of mice and vole" on ironically peaceful "feathery blankets of snow." This violence is nevertheless mitigated, even transformed, by the catalogues of rural objects that run throughout the poems. Through them man re-enters the cycle of nature. "First Hymn" concludes:

> so let's pray again and stamp our worship
> onto stones and rings   let the earth smile
>
> and let us rise like good bread
> baked from sour mash   and wholesome leaven.

Gill, like Thoreau, has a naturalist's eye for startling specific details, and like Thoreau he delights in constantly surprising his readers. Morals come at the most unexpected moments, for example, as pears rot:

> the tree is old
> twisted
> thorny

as the fruit rots
it smells
bugs
birds
all flock
joy
and
economy
where
are you?

In "Cayuga Lake" when two huge carp surface to eat bread,
it is as if the poet's hard-earned insight has given him a
vision of the spirit of nature.

"The Neighbor" section finds him a filter for other voices:
sometimes his own made more remote, sometimes that of
a neighboring farmer, and sometimes, to use Thoreau's
phrase, that of the Original Inhabitant. The poet gains not
only a knowledge of facts but the wisdom to interpret
them, which he does in "Signs." And signs are everywhere
because he has come to know that all things are symbolic.

The poet's progress--and our own--toward such wisdom has
been difficult but joyous. The happiness of sharing a good
book of poetry is not the least of the country pleasures to
which John Gill invites us.

Victor Contoski
Lawrence, Kansas
July 22, 1975

Prologues

I have passed by.
Each day another door like the last
with its simple unadorned face
divorced from the one that opened yesterday
narrower or wider or the paint more sadly flaked
and as I touch the cold knob
I hear a murmur of voices complaining
a faint vacuumed roar
of someone teasing, a hissing sound like a snake.
How is it possible!
the room's perfectly decorous and sane
all squat and bovine comfortable as before
in the neutral commodious light.
Nothing vanishes though I spring forth
no shadows slinking away.
Yet I persist. I attack.
Today, for instance, there was a yellowing American flag
lying in the corner
like a skirt dropped and left where it fell.
As if I'd caught an edge of the dusty terrible
I stood astounded and stupidly confirmed:
my state measured and much too real to tell.

Chicago

I

the backyard
where all things start
exposed iris bulbs cluster and rot in clinker soil
stones, bones, bottles and dog poop
a catalpa tree with sickle thin cigars
we even lit them up and puffed a few
pretending to be someone like adults
there were trees of heaven along the fence
straggly and poor jesus trees they grew anywhere
and one huge shadowing dry elm
that brooded so high it didn't count
until fall when I had to rake leaves.
with smells of molding things and centipedes, beetles,
hundreds of pissy-looking weeds, some rachitic grass
barely hanging on, and a lilac whose blue
so washed out it had to be imagined
blooming, when it did, next to the garbage pail.

once this land was Lake Michigan floor
still sandy, still determined to be itself
a pledged sour rind of earth not to breed
and my earliest life dumped here
a good son of a good son of a good son
who made it from the old homestead farm
and bought this planted victorian house and yard
to hang up his golden plaque: his Doctor's sign
in staid triumph by the door. I've often tried
to conjure up the past that belongs to me but it fails--
two scotch-irish immigrant brothers, one Catesby
with many children in Havana, Ill. while my ghostly fathers
run to Indians camping on this shore
fishing, digging clams, their daily hymns of work and joy
gone, not even rubbled artifacts choked in the soil
but a child-hood honed on bare backyard alkali and weeds.

II

camping out all night in the yard
on the dark furtive ground
wrapped in home blankets to keep us warm
appalled and thrilled at our daring
we took flashlights to warn off robbers and murderers
and food to sustain our lives
(the back door unlocked in case we really got scared)
and sallied out armfuls and armfuls
the lights winking off in the house
our talk dwindled   first quaking at all noise
then less and less trembling as the moon rode free
and night bloomed dreaming its innocence
turned   my friend told me what he'd learned
from another boy--look, it gets big you stroke mine
I'll stroke yours
such palm shock such a depth spinning buzz
seized and sent floating by heels
hot hands taking turns: wonderment   disbelief
that such sensations were invented
it was this then that all parents hid!
flesh-dyed wrong but true guttural song
a winding tenuous stony terrible delicious thread
thieves and murderers stamping their way out of the ground
the moon fluttering in calm disbelief over our exposed bodies
drifting from our seed bed   ripped open   dreaming.

III

my sister and her girlfriend left the light on late
I could see it spooning out under the door
along with the murmur and the laughter
and imagined them in their slips smoking cigarettes
girdles and garterbelts thrown on the floor
and hairpins scattered like shot and close feminine odor
their lips wiped off with bogey cold cream faces
combing or curling their mouse-blonde hair   tee! hee!
and I felt sad and ashamed for them
(my sister guarding small breasts from me
if I saw her by accident in the hall)
nothing ripened or bloomed fully inevitable
no mystery reaching outside their small secret shares
but dead-white shanks and boards creaking at night
they who had always dreamed hollywood faces
calling out, perhaps they were repolishing their nails
calling, so I imagined, piteously, like cats behind damp doors.

IV

I was probably digging to China and almost through
when somebody gave me the exciting news:
a naked woman and a naked man were on the roof
of the apartment house next door five flights up.
I dropped my shovel and scanned the brick horizon
squinting against the sun like Adam after creation
wonder filling every muscle, sac and pore
sprouting visionary senses:
a naked woman breasts swinging as she pranced
her blinding V and her fat bouncing buttocks
and a man his bushy crotch with his flag wagging semaphore
(I knew that they must be drunk)
up on top of the world on the hot tar roof
waving and looking down on the walking dummies below
sedately zipped in their skins flags and negatives furled.
Oh, it was wrong! It was wrong! I mean
to drink and not to be at work (or quiet) in the daytime
and to climb on the roof and prance and shock the neighborhood
to bring the cops to drag them off shouting obscenities!

I never did see them up there although I looked for weeks
scanning that brick horizon faithfully (better than saying prayers)
and entered without knowing it another of Adam's worlds.

Hymn to Thoreau

fog over the river puffs and slides
smooth as a boat drifting and dreaming
Thoreau Henry crabwise married
on God's shelf a redeeming prize
who sent you out without a gun
His morning's classical empire to scrutinize?

arm like the dry branch of a tree
a wood dryad myriad in his leaves
as fiery as fact the holy workings
                    of everysun pushed close
with naked eye: "redeemed on *my* head"
he might say learning garnered and shed.

let's have no shivering no turning away
the Transcendental is woodchuck
                    his black bottom eyes
                    is smoke dead robins
                    the hunched snow pine

ah the sap that flows through cracks in ice
the loon laughs and dives
the squirrels nest the ants dragoon but you!

an experiment in self self-tried and found
home-bound at last and set immortal down

pocketed and put right you lovely/woodshaving/man
may you grow moss where your head now listens and lies.

Notes For A Manifesto

page 1

1st. of all let's worship the gods
the gods of country pleasures
Priapus   Diana   Dame Nature
the minor deities
rustic airs and graces
all natural life
particulars   fiery symbols
and blessed figures

you are cold and cooling?
(notice how a drop of water
or a tear will stick
before it slides)
why   burrow deeper
borrow a hoe or a rake
for yr. own garden
or tend yr. furnace
or watch yr. cat
lick itself nervously
harnessed energy
like a ball
turned and smoothed
its cat-nature
can a cat despair--like you?

page 2

old blind Priapus
that cock
that limber
that muscle
that musk
that catacomb fighter
that slippery bough
that forward furrow
that bottom plower
that testy fellow
sly winker (dumb spurt thinker)
oh, flesh weighty
hand harrowed
bountiful   beautiful
jumping jupiter
drive home to hammer
throw nets to matter
lilting in sorrow
easing to aching
to pucker and wear
to lovely weather
to you now
to the presence of now

page 3

Diana   she calls
herself   Diana
and the deer bounds
the rabbit wrinkles
the squirrel scatters
nut-shards on the ground

Diana is an inland breeze
she turns fields into dry waters
that wave and roar

she has cold fingers

she is chaste   or so the legend goes
(no-one has seen her)

she has infinite grace

She is lovely as evergreens
as misty white clouds
on rolling hills

her resting place is by the pond
where the grass shivers
the willows silvery in the shade

page 4

Dear Dame Nature
you are another
kindly call us together
on our isolate farms

the tractors plow all nite long
their lights like companionable stars
winking at the end of the furrow
earth plowed and disced   mealed
ready for seed

into yr. belly then   shot hard
no easy life for you or for me

Prologue

the exact spot
who knew where he was
a gaggle of geese
in a loose fitting wedge
pools of snow-water forming
hard bright days of February
seeming to know   slipping in and out

the cat is nervous   she jerks
the dog has taken to howling at the moon
in early morning   some belly agony
that it knows and doesn't know
and what to say of the walls of honesty
we built all winter?
does the wall sing now?

like a crowd of eunuchs open-mouthed
tons of mud pouring over the falls
in an endless mighty blast
and the sweet almost sickly smell
of earth and oil along the highway
animals smeared or broken-backed

all the crud of getting there
left behind in the exhaust
the exact spot   found   to move in

Country Pleasures

Something More Ghostly

This is not an unkind land
upstate New York
Finger Lakes Region
where glacial lakes keep their cold
til mid-july
and rocky canyons bring the water down
past great falls and cliffs of shale
to fill bony fingers:
Skaneateles, Owasco, Cayuga, Seneca, Canandaigua
ghostly names still treading the past
not used--"recreation areas," hopefully, on the map
where early bright empire cities
Elmira, Binghamton, Bath,
Geneva, Watkins Glen, Aurora, Auburn. . .
their Victorian grace and gimcrack gentility
linger in a faint smell of dust,
a few streets, or the way the light is sometimes laid
grey and nostalgic like the heartless past
of Empire and Sullivan's stolid march and rape
where even his men, their war-whoops of joy
less commanding, grew tired of destroying
such quantities abounding:
tons and acres of corn piled and burnt.

Delightful peach and apple orchards girdled.
Villages wiped out so the savages won't come back.
No adventure left, his raiders saw the land
returned to divide and farm and speculate.
"Why, them Indians had fine log houses
windows filled with something looked like glass.
Better than what I had back East!"
So we came
where even now we camp on conquered ground
right off the highway
and something more ghostly rings us in
a restlessness, a vague fear, a distaste
as simple as the weather
for this quietly spectacular land
whose ancient people, Seneca, meant "people of stone."
The stones remain.

What of...

what of radishes lettuce peas
lifting out of the hard ground!
and if you could hear the strain of labor
or even imagine the unimaginable pressure
on the bent backs of the bean!
all night soaking in sweat of dew
on the mother-bedded exhaling acres
stars pricking the future above them
while worms chew and grubs curl inward
roots spreading in stony underkeep.
then the sun diffusing a bluish light
then wave on wave mounts and shoots
vociferous to their patient sheds of green
a blinding hallelujah of fire
and yes yes yes to possibility.

3-16-66

the north side of the roof holds its frost
       til almost noon
the grip of heaviness is my lament the pain
       that so insists
winter, ride over, can't your breath lift
       in a pure arc?
but the frost congeals and clots every night
       the mud is stiff
there are some green spikes that pierce the snow
       the pinkish tint
of rhubarb still closed tight in a fist
       is ready to grow
but spring is so begrudging it hurts my chest
       everyone is sad
their breath lifts into a strange lament
       the world will come
but the birth is hard the pangs agonizingly slow.

Late Spring

the swallows flap in waves against the house
they 'chit-chit' nervously trying to nest
      under the roof of the porch
      in the rafters of the garage
      anyplace under the wide eaves
and the house rides high in the deep green sea
and robins row sporadically in the calm
and catbirds cry to their soulful mates
and the field sparrow sitting straight up on a spar
      singing land ho! on lookout
and dirty starlings prowl and poke beaks
      eyes gleaming for creamy eggs
and the yellow warbler in cheerful toil
      sweeps the deck of bugs and insects
he stares into the cabin where I sit and read
and meadowlarks, blackbirds, bobolinks spread
rising and falling to the horizon as the ocean heaves
while over us all our albatross the mighty hawk
stiffly circles and spirals catching the exhalations
of heat, cries, movement, sweat, turning them to account
as he glides, almost free, in his heaven above the waves
and we sail we sail rooted by his lightning
            sheathed and unsheathed.

something broke the dream
turned him over   the sun in his eye
to silence   a nearby tree sighed
or was it a chorus of boys
shrill in the distance
"the eye, the eye, the honeyed eye!"

he was staring in the mirror
& from under his upper lid
a small moist stirring
then a grey moth appeared
small as a tear it squeezed out
& flew away   then 2 more insects came
one of them a sleek wasp
& finally 2 fat-bellied bees
pushed their heads & forelegs out
popping out before drawing back in

oh, the hidden pollen of his eye!
bees making him their hive
the others escaping
the taste of their possible honey
like ripe fruit bruised
his dreaming mouth.

First Hymn

for A.M. Klein

anything that promises   good
day   night   summertime   pregnant evil

do come   do come easier

the West brings storms and cutting wind
cables snapt and shingles blown

by South   the distant South   arrows
tipped dive into sun-beached haven

while North the big cream slowly spreads
white and blank   as mad as chaos

and Brother East yawns on his wide bed
promising what we know is foolish from heaven

so let's pray again and stamp our worship
onto stones and rings   let the earth smile

and let us rise like good bread
baked from sour mash   and wholesome leaven.

Taughannock Gorge

every spring they trip in
drunk and mad at their girl
on the old railroad bridge
waving their arms and threatening
as she looks on

or else they back up
from the fire built
too close to the edge
their graduation fling
ending in the stream bed
their friends open-mouthed
in the embers' glow

or else they shake off
that one step that ties
them to despair
and plummet soundlessly
into the rapids below

or if they're old
and more brittle-boned
they've done it already
in much less dizzy air
gathered caution about them
and God only knows
why they're standing here.

Long Time No

the frontiers keep changing
it's white roses in late September
blooming in the ditch
dead skin from the underworld
hand of a queen or a beautiful witch
rising out of the ground
not that you'd want to fall on her breast
she is odorless/tired/not-to-be-touched
not enticing a bit: she puts her hand out
like condensed smoke
I think she's "Wilhelm Kaiserina"
Prussian bred   fancied by those who fancy roses
I think the Kaiser bred her
I can see him stomping around
enjoying his garden
quite fond of her late in life
as he was earlier of changing frontiers
all things change: today
it's winter wrens and creamy sparrows.

11-8-70

I pruned the honeysuckle bush today
cut it back severely
and clipt the climbing rose
so it won't scratch my study window
all winter   more open space and bleak sun

the sparrows look unhappy
their old honeysuckle perch stripped--
like convicts in a country courtyard

but I prefer cutting back
to cut the winter's cold

the loss is more focused
the sap can pool its heavy load.

Complaint

everything gives me away
crass pumpkin flower
the swollen bee
swallows dipping to the wire
trees rocking their leaves

everything croons to me   of him
are off-shoots of desire
full to bursting

the pomegranate on the table
its encased jewel-seeds
sit and spit at me.

Meat

the steer has been slaughtered
it lies on the ground   legs up
it has been decapitated--a knobbly
red mushroom stump where the head was

a strip of hide about 6 inches wide
has been peeled from throat to belly
it dangles over the flank
like a sash

two men stand looking down

i'm sure they see the same things
neat packages in the freezer
steaming meat on the table

but now they hesitate

the powerful chest and carcass
legs stiff as an invitation
or as a supplication
to something   indecent

the headless steer bellowing
like thunder from the ground
making them worshippers
calling them fools

it only lasts a moment
before they get down to business

stripping   gutting   sawing
the inevitable blood bath.

late at nite
the owls of December snow
"Who-Ah-Who-Who-Who"
from their perch
on the evergreens
faces turning
like clocks not
missing a beat
(or rather a scent)
of the subtle pleasures
that are out wandering
tiny purses of mice and vole
are their gathering
and their doing good
their harvest of beatitude
where terror and necessity meet
talons outstretched
on feathery blankets of snow.

Rural News

at the end of a severe winter
(mother dead
father dead
sisters & brothers all gone)
under 18 blankets
a W.W.I. army greatcoat
6 sweaters   2 work shirts
3 pairs of pants   2 pairs of woolen socks
& one pair of dirty longjohns
he was found dead in his parents' bed
by neighbors
who   when all things sniff outofdoors
wondered why he didn't appear
& lift his face cautiously
to the faint twinge of spring.
instead   he marched the other way
to an ever-narrowing measure
& foetal ledge as cold as his source
& as putridly stale as the fates
who arrange such scenes.

Litany

Preacher:	floating from the tree of life I see strangers in every garden waiting for God to strike
Response:	bodies so greedy they pull in all directions
P.	more than the sun in its path more than the moon in its phases star-lit in intensity
Res.	a hole in every roof where the smoke pours out or like roots in the form of children buried in the earth their cries smothered
P.	who is there that understands? who has the patience and the delicacy? who can forget long enough to care?
Res.	and is there a season and a place?
All:	or are we crazy unformed burnt-out living from the tip of our noses savoring the smell at the edge of the burning garden?

Hymn to Winter Sparrows

may your body lice freeze in the cold
and pepper the snow

may the softness and warmth of your feathers protect you

may you gather on the leeward side of the house
to banter the news   all that you can tell

may you find bread and suet in your path

may the hawks, the cats, and the crows suddenly get cataracts

may the nights but promise a new day
as you roost under the eaves
your dreams nesting in summer   leafy and green

and may you wake   bold and shining   sunny as brass
heads clear   eyes bright
ready to take on the world

whatever's been decently deposited
whatever comes your way.

March

notice how the crows uplift
and drift as they beat
across the snow-stubbled field

in the mouth of March
what darkness covers?
what nets are thrown over us?

the more you keep combing it
the more falls out
dry   like the sound of surf

one foot crosses the other
as if it needed weight
to drive the other down

ice-forms slide and grumble
raucous like the hens
penned in the henhouse

the lead sky lightens behind
itself too bright
almost for weak eyes

twigs bushes trees
are bent and ugly
only their patience shines

what are the dogs doing
all night long
prowling the limits of the farm?

like pebbles in the mouth
like what cannot rush
like this horn of song.

Before the Thaw

for Lyn

have you seen me   at all
riding country roads
right down the center

the blinding light from the snow
everywhere
going to milk barns to buy milk raw

or looking out at the barns
from the "study" window
just waiting
for them to collapse forever

Indian ghosts underground
suburbs advancing in shock waves

the highway belting along from the city
taking that corner field of evergreens

the hawk reduced from the dead tree
by the pond

if so   you already know
what I mean about country pleasures
and are waiting   like me   for the thaw

to stand compared

life is very fast
for little birds
one
sits on a wire
flick flick flick
hot seed
shutter tail
its blood is
bug ichor
& water
puff bones
& feathers
dry twig feet
it rocks
it holds
sips
air
the invisible
sweet
all things
make it
quiver
now now
to dart
after
to stay
it thrills
it registers
i get dizzy
have to
turn
away

Mr. Sims Comes Home

I am home again
after a major operation
pale, snail-like, blankly
sitting in my chair.
You, who suffered
through my hospital agonies
alone, suddenly hate me,
my remoteness, my stitches,
my dull, animal stare.

"I am unhappy, my life
is garbage, you don't want
a wife, etc."   I grind
my jaw--incredulous.
I had forgotten love,
that other pain
opening its prickly heart
the raw wound burning
smartly in the air!

Explanation

politics is on the other shore
across the lake
with the dotted red and white lights
of the County Airport.
sometimes, if it's a dry fall,
flames from a distant grass fire
cast lights and shadows
like a giant dumb-show
against the hills
--it's exciting but pretty far away.

nostalgia

sickle pears
are tiny russet
hard fruit
fit to pickle
not to eat
hardly anyone
knows the recipe
anymore
the birds
however
wet their beaks
in the pulp
a neat drink
on a hot day
right now
an oriole
velvet-orange-black
is plundering
the tree is old
twisted
thorny
as the fruit rots
it smells
bugs
birds
all flock
joy
and
economy
where
are you?

The Old Farmer

at 92 he weakened a bit
instead of bouncing to town in his jeep
he took to walking the fields in early spring
cap and muffler on   his quiet breath
flowing before him like a trail

his wife had been recently buried
his sons and daughters old and scattered

the pond was his favorite lingering spot
as though staring at the past
he'd stand at the edge of the water

the pond seemed to stare with him
benign old cloudy rain-pool matter
perhaps they both saw something--

watched his unadorned old heart
rise up steaming from the bottom
and pump its way slowly to shore

like a giant frog pocked and ancient
the granddaddy of all these inland waters

How to Keep Yr. Mother Alive

there's no way to prolong this feathery life
except by being feathery
and it's nobody's business
that you live with her
yr. back room full of newspapers and glass jars
isolation so embracing it makes you blush
when you trim yr. toenails

it started innocently enough
tickles in the bath   wiping yr. runny nose
now it's feathery and hard   like coral

and it's spread everywhere

the world is almost not real
or so with a distant vengeance
and what can you do

there are leaks and proofs   of course
of other modes of living
the bottle   a fear of heights
dizziness that overtakes you playing poker
you reach for yr. watch and make excuses

it's hard mothering at yr. age
but she's used to you   benign

and what she's given are strokes
so indelible and patient that time
like the pretty boy who never ran away
is always there   loving and waiting.

Everything is half-exposed
9 spokes is now 13 above the snow
on the vegetable garden wheel--
bushes bent and cracked from winter rise
and all the tools we lost: rakes
shovels, trowels suddenly appear
where they were dropped last fall.

I am not capable of gluttony.
My wife, my children, my friends rise
even sparrows--those flea bags of intensity--
sit quietly in the vines against the wall
where the sun catches them and shines
with such rounding relentlessness
that if I could pray otherwise I would:
drive me out decently or else cover and close.

there is a center to the woods
where only kids and poets out walking
ever come   it's not easy to reach
you have to cross three fields
scratch your way through raspberry tangle
push through hardwoods   before you hear
the brook rush   smell the ozone air
and enter the primitive world
of ferns and mosses breathing as it has
for lost millions of years
with sweet flowers everywhere
fringed polygala like baby orchids
nodding dutchman's-breeches   bloodroot
hairy hepatica and wild ginger
dog-tooth violets and spring beauty
at each step downstream more
you touch nearer the total green
shy colors massing   the heart of your country

2 teen-age gas attendants...

abducted and shot in the groin
by the mad sex-killer
a dimpled man with a mustache
and a pacific leer

oh herd them in honey
and sting them to death

never shall they dare
never shall they steal from you

as the wheels roll over the bell
and the boys come running to wipe and to fill

you enticed them oh yes yes
waving it in their eyes
til they got in

til they were blind with the joy of it
blood and powder smeared on the seats
the end of it

crowing and driving like hell
with your hot cargo over the faraway hills.

Luckily the Animal

we walked through the woods to the garbage dump
in early spring   she had been lying on the couch all day
not exactly complaining but I could tell. . .
I gave her tea and cinnamon toast before we left
the dogs went with us--underfoot   the stream was wild
the break-up had begun with cracks and groans
slabs scraping the banks trying to get out
the wind still smacked of snow   its metallic taste
I didn't hold her hand or anything like that
we just walked through the woods to the dump
in early spring not saying anything
nothing needed to say.

5-7-69

wld. you believe it
she's kneeling on the ground   hunched over
   pulling weeds from the old strawberry bed
   it's cold for May & damp
   it's been raining & it's abt. to rain

her hair falls in her face
   she separates   pulls
   & throws the weeds over her shoulder
   continuous   small   flying motions

squat   muddy   at home
   a woodchuck beside its burrow
   never took so sweet a day

"What do you want?" I said.
the night all almond flowered.
"You've got a smudge on yr. cheek," I said
& tried to rub it off.
her skin felt cold-smooth to my fingers.
I kissed both cheeks   her nose
her lips--just tasted
did not enter in.

And what did I expect?
eternal youth!
to be a flaming Bodhisattva
the lotus under my heels
my heels carpeted above the waters!

I am a flaming Bodhisattva.
I touched her cheek   all almond flowered.
kissed her mouth.
entered the flaming waters
my heels floating above the carpet.

What did I expect
the night being almond shaped & flowered?

Wild Water

Where's the wild slapping waves rocky and grunt?
So far inland   valley of the quiet cup
cricket-hearth   peepers' song   ear-thrid humming
of the caves and coves where oceans breathe.

Once sharks swam the Kansas seas
their cold joy triumphant   wickering
and glaciers ground   relentless   these fields
now drained   now soft-burred and chewy.

So still   the fog steams up like flower-burst
and the deer step timid   backward in time.
Blackbirds rise in a heavy-pursed rush
to settle further away   to close the day down.

Later the moon will hunch over the pines
owls will string their monotonous reveries
and I will walk home   oar across my shoulder-blades.

Trying to Feed the Black Rooster

you hook a hand to your eye to see straight
there's nothing on the path but red comb honey and black ire
as sounding a weight as ever thrown into the sea to suck back
once the bell of revolt's been sounded   being colonialist
and rational you hesitate determining strategy
but with a rush and whirr and gallop of wings it's on you
apocalypse of what you deserve   your committed fate
to go down rigid and stumbling saying "is this me!"
still not knowing the answer   gifts still clenched in your hand
the rooster crowing and clapping treading ribbons of blood
                                                    overhead
his eyes closed in ecstasy   his bony malevolent features
your free hand hooked to his comb as red as the sea

Farmer

getting up to the land
naked in his picture window
he peers out at the misty fields
across the road
steaming like dung in early light.
almost ripe to plow!
day come round again.

I zap by in my drive
to nowhere and see him
like a camera click   go by.
a holy flushed jolt!
original Adam   waking

fingers peel my brow
apple flesh firm and bright.

Country Register

who killed the rooster
with the crippled claw?
he died in a pool of blood
bottoms up
protecting his hens

what happened to Blinky
the beagle that disappeared
one fall day?
hot on a scent
he whipped into the woods

and those tiny bones
on a nest of pine needles
deep in the evergreens
where the sun never comes
what   were   they?

and the hawk in the tree
the great horned owl
the silly woodcock
the bittern by the pond
did they just   fly away?

not to mention the old
bright as buttons
puttering in their gardens
secure in their savings
where are they?

and the young farmers
sent to Vietnam
to fight for their country
are they gone
in the bowels of war?

and the suicides?
their bodies pile up
like snowdrifts
in the newspapers
those drained white faces

and those killed by accident?
pinned beneath the tractor
fallen from the silo
or whose charred remains
smoulder in the fire

and the generations
raised for slaughter
the cattle and the fowl
the heaps of dead
casually washed away?

they all   come   knocking
at the country register
not so much demanding
as here to stay.

Fantasy Life

"I'm the devil, here to do the devil's work,"
Watson said--before the blood bath at the Tate house
woman in a white gown running bloodied path
thumps, groans, funny things happening--
couldn't get the knife in   kept hitting bone & hurt my hand
head-ache--the victim pulled my hair so hard she complained
blood all over the place had to hose the car down
we'll show them the way it should be done
"Do you know who I am?" said Manson
didn't explain   just twirled her around
a cross scratched on his forehead

"Have hot 8 inch   make a date"
"Want young well-hung boys to suck: 7/31/75 at 2:00 pm."
"Show it hard"   a crude hole between stalls
arrows pointing to a mouth

"Sanctify thy shit," said the poet Clay

obsolete nerve gas will be shipped
then dumped 1500 ft. deep in the ocean   250 miles out
scientists spent a year figuring the best way. . .

the grand jury find that the police were justified
into the girls' dorm   150 rounds   2 dead
"Power To The People," Nixon said straight-face
at the 1st. live televised news conference he ever held
outside the White House
his right hand shooting out in a little open-palm
half-gesture from the hip

I give her pleasure   she gives me pleasure
it's rained for a week   my chair is sticky
I smoke too much   drink too much coffee
in the country where I live

it really takes time to kill
a furry spider

covered a delicate-winged nervous fly
in a death-grip   or so I thought
I brushed them apart
surprised to find the fly unhurt
the spider so disengaged

"What is reality?" the pupil asked the Master

"I am afraid," counterweight pulling the pan down
"I am abandoned,"   No Reaction   see the I Ching
Full Moon Rising Above The Lake

Country Isolation

a male pheasant skitters
through deep falling snow
in the garden
his tail swerving in an arc
as he runs into the field
no food!   no females!
open territory!
my dogs snooze
near the stove
I look out the window
think   how silly he looks
enjoy his bronze his red
carnival colors
wonder
where is his rendezvous
in this weather
closing in?
is he late?
with whom will he sit down to eat?

Apology

I could start very quietly
like a needle through cloth
hills & fields of plain stitching. . .

maybe I've loved too cautiously

never put my hand
where my heart flowered
my mind stopped

but turned away

maybe I've been too final
condemned by my own laws
so that now. . .

what you say & what I say
are lessons we repeat
no marriage   but plenty of vows

I could start very quietly
like a snail through snow. . .
hills & fields of wading.

the pleasures of life enter
allright   good enough to see
red-buds in spring   crows lazing
just name it   it's there
ten digits multiplied by ten million
and then some   incredible gifts
given to our senses
easy as breathing
in and out boundlessly
so that   really   we are stars
in our stations   constantly
victims of light and light-giving
poor mortality to be hung so high
what else could we be   but happy!

3
boys strip
& prance
by the edge
of the woods
white buttocks
tiny genitals
tee! hee!
look at me!
bodies to the wind
blowing
softly
sunmelting
on chest
& thighs
flash of
dead pan
one eye
open &
grinning
at
young
baby boys
getting into
the old dance
exposed
downy bodies
giggling
by the edge
of the forest
in the
tall
meadow grass
the old old
dance

see them
tentative
but fast
as summer
comes
the full
shattering thrust
oh   pan
raised up
grinning
dance
dance
for all
your tired
bones

it's spring
someone has burnt off
a plot of grass
near the road
an empty steam-shovel
jaws open to crop char
some cinder blocks stacked
nearby have tumbled
from groundswell
or mere haste of endeavor
no time to stack more
nor to do anything
properly
winter still on our backs
tough old hide under us
and the sun
rolling crazy
in our eyes

Bluegrass Nite at Kosmos

say hello, blossom, say hello to me.

there are times when i'm so far away
fields full of flowers & none of them mine

say hello, blossom, say hello to me

Annie was a gentle one
with a laugh both cutting & wild

Jeanie was a dark one
with eyes eloquent & sad

And Nancy was a silly one
full of flirt & WOW & DAMN

say hello, blossom, say hello to me.

there are times when i'm so turned away
fields full of flowers & none of them mine

not Annie   not Jeanie   not Nancy   no-one
flowers that wave & nod in the sun
flowers that wave & nod in the sun.

not Annie   not Jeanie   not Nancy   no-one

say hello, blossom, say hello to me.
say hello, blossom, say hello to me.

the surge close to the skin   of 21 yrs.   today
Matt   it's yr. song   shy smile   washing dishes at Kosmos

we brought fresh rhubarb pie   I picked cherry blossoms
still wet   with little clots of rain

the rhubarb is delicious   tongue-pink & astringent
the blossoms although dead-white are high & musky

we hope you enjoy them on yr. birthday   Matt
now that you've crossed over   & it's official

the rhubarb is for pleasure even though it puckers yr. face
the blossoms   ah   they're   for the lifting   of the veil.

Elaine

depression's gulch
fleas of sorrow
wherever you are brooding at the time
are like birds in their rumply feathers
on the wire unable to sing
lacking instinct to fly
shifting from one tender perch
to another
no south to harbor or to haven

are there no gifts possible
to take you?
like the hawk takes the sparrow
in one swoop
now that depression has you
glued to its hollow
glued to its drumming hide.

first it's pussy-willow fur
metal gray as the surface of the pond
but stroke it to silver and pollen dust
from there it's a short trip to universal green

birds fly out of every pie
headed for home
they climb in the spiral of yr. eye

you fall asleep
to the old pond sucking its gums
peepers' pulse
the deeper bass of frog

and wake exposed by a merciless moon
its blade at yr. throat
and on yr. belly

nowhere but nowhere
floating
rudderless and high

Jars of

jam that his Mother made
on the shelf
& his Mother dead.
should he eat the jam?
watch it mold?
or throw it away?
preserve it further?
not likely
& the taste
delicate
jellied crab
tart currant
black caps losing
their flavor
to neutral
to nothing
to bad
faster than
he could ever eat.
he sits at the kitchen table
unutterably sad.

Dick's Trumpet Solo

something
got the old man
sitting on the brick wall
in his winter coat and hat
(even though it's officially spring)
alive again

a possibility and a choice
he wld. be wise not to make
after living it all
wife   kids   home   job

they fell away
like cold rain

now it's
a warm room and a small pension

the wall is hard
the day is brisk

something got the old man
into the mood again

Spring Rain

what could be sad sorrowful leaps of the imagination
rain falling in the garden   on the peonies
on the snowy green hydrangeas   what leaps!
and on the crisp tea roses
tiny fingerling leaps
a suave erasure of thunder   bumbling
swallows weaving low baskets of rain
the damp hearts of flowers opening
later
when it will be day or even the other
not to be mentioned   night
where leaps are   indeed   leaps

toads come out to hug the darker shadows
their soft sacs of skin
pulsing much faster than the night seems

cold rain in the garden and hot hot leaps
I am swimming in my mother's body
I leap   my father leaps
we leap again and again and again.

Supplementary List for Travellers

patience like
grass from a dog's stomach
as hard as moth-balls

pieces of sleep
its broken sharp edges

some soapy rain water
beard shavings   pubic hair

a whistle that wheezes
before it blows

something rolled-up & dry

some large figs
small tweezers

a face or two for every occasion

a stick of incense
(how to keep it from breaking?)

the cheerfulness & efficiency of a bank clerk

plus a secret boy-scout stride
to keep you moving

since you never know
who will greet you
or when you will arrive

Cayuga Lake

where is the body but going out in waves
the little girl was calling up something
out of the steel-grey bowels of the lake
washing her doll holding it under too long
doesn't she know it will drown

her fascination with what's under
then she threw bread on the water
came running back to say a huge fish
came back to our laughing doubts

come see what she has called up from the water
the huge fish that we doubted was there

2 golden-brown carp with embossed scales
whirlpooled the water   rose to the bread
leisurely eating & turning to eat again

male & female moving like one & its shadow
like golden rocks in the murk rising to break
eyes   snout   gaping as they ate
backing & tracking on lacy fins

yet so marmoreal so dream-contained they swirled
we all threw bread & exclaimed
come see the huge fish in the water

young & old excited   come see what we have raised!

Pieces of Flint

for Harley Elliott

his hands were tuned to them
right in my neighbor's cornfield
he'd bend and pick them up
rub the dirt off
bring them alive

March was heading toward April
mud gucking our boots
we scoured the fields
had visions of Indian camps
with perfect arrowheads
miraculously spent at our feet

but found instead pieces of flint
he'd examine their virtues
point them out to me
a strong wind blowing
hawks riding the upper currents
a few flap-sided crows passing

when he left I put the flints
on the window sill
where they sit as trophies
their power unknown
to everyone who passes by

unless they stop   look
out at the fields
and start dreaming
then they pick the pieces up
warm them in their hands
and see things worth keeping.

My Life With Ties

I used to wear them
but now my son does
he found a boxful in the closet
my "past life" now that I'm free & poor
& dirty & live in the country
& seldom go to town & when I do
I wear sweaters pull my hair back
in a pony tail & stalk through the streets
saying fuck you 9 to 5 fuck you Capitalism
but my son likes them
he's 13 brushes his hair
puts on clean clothes for school
& wears ties a different one each day
he's at the age that sneers at girls
but has found himself in mirrors
& has to like what he sees
me, I'm near the top of the climb
ties are colored bits of cloth
that flutter before my eyes--I mean
I get nostalgic when I see them
remember certain ones certain days
they hit me in the face sometimes
almost like a dead fish might
the beige & pink-striped one
my son wears today is my wedding tie!
it cost me $10 in 1954
I bought it in a ritzy shop on 5th. Ave.
& was late for my wedding
when I tell him this
he looks at it fingers it & takes it off
but that's not what I meant
I didn't want to burden him with my ties!
maybe he respects the past--me--
history does have a certain weight
so, he's right to drape it over
the dining-room chair & walk away
I can't do that
why in the hell did I put them in a box
& pack them away?
I could have thrown them out anytime.

Neighbor

Neighbor

he embraced a stone once
loved its stony smoothness
its non-life so cold to the touch
what agonies of indecision and of fire
held him I don't know

but I listen when he talks
his talk so full of emptiness
as if he'd crackt the stone
and climbed in to sleep
his arms around the whole world.

he said

when I was young
I was hot as a firecracker
as a steaming teapot
on a hot summer day
a clammy perspiring steam engine
put me in the sun I'd smoke
prelude to a 4-alarm fire
nothing   but nothing cld. damp my blaze

but now   well I've been married 40 yrs.
a bit dryer   you might say
laundry flapping on the line
bleached out   ready to put away.

he said

the old chicken barn
caved in one nite
during a storm
blew its top
now it just gapes
a real eyesore
it'll have to decay
at its own speed
can't afford to rebuild
every time I look
there it is
mocking me
its blank windows
floating timbers
its damp rot
to be philosophical
about it   is hard
everything buckles
at some pt. on the line
we think   ah   ha
we're riding the arrow
when the arrow is riding us.

he said

what once pushed me with such weight
and pooled me so that I was afraid
lessens now   a frantic black wasp
follows me around the house

I am its spirit journey or it is mine
we're both amazed when we meet

I offer it an edge of paper to coax it
lightly as I can out the door

when it hits the sun
it steadies and flies away.

he said

I read in the papers
there is a new breed
of poison-resistant super-rats
developed in the cities and farms
immune to chemicals that wld.
wipe out a population.
they breed and spread
at the rate of 6 to 8 miles
of territory yearly.
they're being dealt with
by a new super-poison
ball. . .where will it end!

our extremities gnawed off
our weak eyes twitching
as we roll in the dust and filth.
and the super-super-rats
you know the ones I mean
become ever more inaccessible
behind their pneumatic doors--
the money closing in.

he said

I lay down in the blizzard
and it snowed white hairs on me.

he said

I hate clarity
I hate light
it robs me
nothing is that firm
or if it is explodes
in the flash
of a thousand suns
sucked back through
black holes in the universe

it comes & goes like breath
it's dark & light
the spirit is watery
a nail of light
in a translucent sac
of birth & of death

there is always something withheld
we made love
& as we rocked to a climax
I found myself hanging on to her
like a ledge
& as I peered into the abyss
I saw space so profound
so thin & empty
I knew I could never come back
yet here I was
a baby again
hanging on
from what world
to what world?
it frightened me.

sitting at his desk on a winter morning
looking out at the frozen landscape
he said

dry stalks
how I'd like to get rid of them
these bars on the winter fields
that drive the cold home.
seeds have left their chambers
seams split   pods burst
the spirit buds have dropt in the snow
or safe in the craw of birds
are shat and spread
some catch in animal fur
then hibernate all winter
to spring again
but these dry stalks
like the ghosts of Cayuga Indians
how I hate them
reminding me of the dead
the cold unwavering dead.

he said

there is a pristine center
did you ever see mist
that's not quite rain
on the window?
or a flame with
a clear filmy peak
between the lower blue
and the sulphur yellow
that's burning?

I see it in people, too
the eyes mostly
when self is cleared away.
there's no touching it
that's for warmth or need.
this is beyond that
anterior to time
shooting from the galaxies

a light so diffuse and intense
that words can't hold it
it's there stubborn as grit
it contains us
bores us right through
yes, indeed.

he said

Time does not do
anything. It is done.

It does not flow
or pass.

It is always full
always present.

It's everywhere
like sleep filling the room.

It is dreadful
as well as enticing.

You keep wanting
to trip it up
out-run it
before it gets away.

The pulse that beats
under covers is your own.

It has no taproot
yet it cracks foundations
with its hairs.

It almost never blinks
yet it is a signal
palms up on the table.

It is not the Mother
but it could be her shadow
there when you nod

ready to catch you
when you fall.

Signs

Feb. 10, 1975

it's cold
there's light snow on the ground
4 people are standing near a grave
in the middle of a cemetery
they are the highest verticals around
they look like they're waiting for a bus
they've left space at their feet
for the 5th. one buried there
2 of them are looking down
1 of them is seeing something
they are all waiting
will someone speak?
they are motionless
there is nothing to say.

Feb. 13, 1975

lady-bug crawling
out of yr. hatch
ahoy & clear sailing
yr. red is persuasive
yr. black dots mysterious
sign that yr. loved
have been thought out
completely
down to yr. stubby
encapsuled wings
that bear so much freight.
all yr. kitchen worries
yr. sing-song tragedies
yr. destiny
here on my wrist.
oh, fly away
fly away
go, fly away
home.

Feb. 15, 1975

following old deer tracks in the snow
dogs & I startled a rabbit
it took off in a heat
dinky is old she just blinked
little gusty didn't even see it
I wasn't amused watching it zig-zag tail
going bippedy-bip through the snow
I was shadowing deer in my head
thinking abt. the coming together
of all their separate trails
somewhere in these woods the deer
have nests where they bend their haunches
ruminate & softly stare
rounded-out places under pine
where their breath rises in sociable steam
their flanks the color of dried grass
I'd watch them awhile
then prop my back against their sides
settle among them to rest
and then!   and then!
maybe I'd be satisfied
with myself & with my day.

March 12, 1975

a dry "kreeetch" ½-way between
a cough and a wheeze
comes from the snow-ball bush
in the yard followed by a "clack."
and I know the blackbirds are here.
something has told them to return
in this dismal freezing cold.
but it's more like a joke
they cough and wheeze
hop up and down
shivering on their perch
no huddlement in sight
no waving luscious weeds
just bitter wind and driving snow.

that's the trouble with being first:
there you are.

though I must admit
since their return
I keep hearing water running
underneath everything
and a movement so very faint
almost like vertigo
that jostles threatens
to pull me into the current
creeping above my ankles
and higher higher
I'll cast off
the trees gold-green
the sun throwing melons of light
oh blackbirds! blackbirds!
and there you are
there you are.

March 24, 1975

the great turtle
has maps of slow voyages
from the cattails in the swamp
across the highway
to the inlet and back
inscribed on its ivory belly
its snake-like head twists slowly
its legs churn like wheels
when I pick it up
and take it off the road
but there's no turning round
the swamp's a baseball diamond now
the inlet's full of boats
I put it in a rain puddle
near the parking lot
to find its way again
the maps changed
its instincts strong.

March 30, 1975

one minute snow blinds the window
          driving slant-past
and wind rattles the limber branches
          puffed and whip-lashed
then suddenly the snow dies
          winds unmount and the sun
          dazzles
          in a crude beginning calm
twice as harsh as winter gone

April 21, 1967

woke up Jim Belou at half-past 4
shook the knob   rattled the door
"tell me   buddy   tell me true
is you lonesome   or isn't you?"

June 28, 1975

in cutting the tangle of raspberry cane
out by the side of the barn
one fresh summer morning
I uncovered a song sparrow's nest
the mother bird brooding tightly
among the shadowy vines her brown
back blended and only her eye
that bright household terror
gave her away   she held
I held   then stepped lightly aside

later   with her cupped in mind
I looked and bent and peered
but no tight mother bird
no tiny cluster of eggs
not even an egg-shell grain

the cats had been at work
eggs spilled and crushed
did she get to the roof
or did she go down
one brief flutter and flash
her bright eye still bright
as trophy-like between the cat's teeth
she held
as he stepped briskly on his way?

July 20, 1975

July is like a honeycomb
sunflowers thump at the door
yr. body & my body pile up
murderous & lovely
so shallow-breathed
so packed with seed.

August 8, 1975

tonite the sky is like a big animal
by that I don't mean the wily bear
is squinting at the earth
to catch us in his claws
although I'm sure he could
put us in harness if he liked
crack us across his back
where we'd ride forever.

maybe I've been looking too long!
the sky is like a huge animal
glinting and dangerous
cradling the earth.
we could lose keel
easily in such a nite
not know if we were plunging up
or down losing all track.
as it is I stagger on
shot through with hot eyes
hoping to find the right door.

August 22, 1975

where are they going?
small-town girls
walking the outer reaches of Main St. alone
the country is about to start
will they slip between rows of corn
turn into thick-braided Indian squaws
and lie down giggling?
I doubt it
are they meeting boys in the cemetery
to hold hands in the rain
pale and tense
mothers and fathers all around them?
perhaps
but most likely they will walk
in a loose circuit threading back home
demure heads down stuffed with flight
like the moon tonite
whipped between clouds.

Sept. 19, 1975

tomatoes ripening slower now
apple-green & snowy-orange
a few tell-tale red
splitting juicy seams to be pickt
& carried in my shirt
almost as delicately as eggs
to the house
small domestic virtues triumph
sitting in a chair in the sun
near the great spruce tree
small fires & glints still burn
within an intense calm
catbirds meow in the bush
here they are   hanging on
& I thought they had left
but no   that deeper hum
rises from the fields
& circles us here

sickle moon tonite cupped
at the end of the road
like a woman's breast
hung in darkest shadow
walking is like swimming
in this absence
cool & inviting
a woodcock whirrs to nest
in the high field
a truck comes by
white lights   red
voices flashing
over the grinding of gears
waving hello   goodbye
it's all the same song.

October 13, 1975

small sprig of bachelor buttons
on my desk. blue. pink. white.
maverick purple. small heads
leaning stiffly against nite
& cold

oh Coleridge you look down
with yr. heavy-lidded pain

what hope is there?
what hope is there

put into words
& colors held up

Nov. 19, 1975

he parked his car
he stepped around it slowly
he was middle-aged
he held himself like in those ads
for sore and aching muscles
but here in the grey light
of upstate New York winter
nothing could bring relief
not even a trip for the mail
and so he manuevered himself
by walking slowly
past my fenders holding up
his crossed face as a model
born of necessity and fate
like the weather itself
leaking light on the road
like the green cinder-block P.O.
like the stripped trees and dead grass
like the several clapboard houses
planted here and still sounding
like some weary fact
like timeless time making motions
in the vast nasty
like my hands on the steering wheel
leaning forward
like his pain
like mine seeing
like everyday miraculous
too true almost
to be believed.

Nov. 29, 1975

riding down Cemetery Road
passing cornfields and houses
coming up a slight rise
Smith woods on the left
the cemetery grounds on the right.
pretty as a picture with trees
lots of bushes and countless rows
of headstones from great big to little
straight and tilted some decorated
with plastic flowers and plastic greens
a few ugly crypts
a statue in pensive style
either an angel or a daughter
no birds--it's late November
but even in spring it's quiet here
and lots and lots of names
not just Son and Father and Mother
and Daughter or Beloved
but real soil-smacking names
like Neigh, O'Keefe, Griswold,
Tupper, Vanderhaven and Poole
and I thought almost like I saw
bones pull from the ground
sweeping up and down rows
arms to shoulders to heads
to bodies to legs clacking
up out of those graves
swirling to catch arms
and dance ah ha to dance
it just took a minute
I even saw bonnets on the women
and huge skirts over petticoats
and why not I thought
it's possible it happened
right now even though I looked
and saw acres of headstones
like patient teeth still biting
everybody danced
everybody had a good time.

The Wedding Poem

for Jennifer & Jon at Taughannock Falls
overlook, Aug. 26, 1974

This is the time of year when all that's molten bends
when the sun is full yet soothing
when the hive is soon-to-be honey-delight
when the earth churns   the fields almost ready
insects humming & swelling in a hidden chorus of leaf & shade
when the screech owl cries at nite like a baby
from its perch in the woods
& the moon in the sky is half a blood-pie
that wavers & wanes into pale yellow
following us down the road

Then, I'd say, we're ready (O Lord we are ready)
for the completion   for the act
that will join us   here at the side of the gorge
higher than birds in the sky
at the Great Falls in the Woods
standing on sacred Indian ground
looking at the falls & at the bowl of space beneath it
like an inverted sky with a thread through the middle
letting in & letting out
everything microscopically little & yet not safe
distant & timeless too
as timeless & as human as what pulls us here
today   at the falls   for the joining of Jennifer & Jon

in the big world this is of no consequence
up or down   saving the farm   beauty left

this   silly domestic dull bliss
the hens fretting   the rooster on his toes clapping
to his own challenge   his own mirror

though the racoon at nite dreams warm blood
and is drawn to the henhouse

the sleepy rain   the intense green world
that soaks it up light and shadow and all

so that green becomes another shade of black unfurled
and we become insect-bitten armed swingers of order

here to combat every day devouring life
give it back to itself in shape and law

it is of no consequence   but it is our answer

Hail, Ezra

his back to everyone
he sailed into view
literally
in my dream
slouch hat   baggy clothes
in a small sailboat
he bent over busy
throwing fish
into the sea
the waves were choppy
his footing not firm
he balanced bent & threw
raising his head at the toss
to trace the arc of his aim
the fish were silver scimitars
flashing & sucking under
with a neat flip
he had caught them earlier
I was sure
I could see him worming a hook
but now he was undoing
all that he had done
the salt spray chopping
the rocking boat
flow of constant motion
the sail spanking & flapping
his old but vigorous
frame & bent back
hail to you   Ezra
true to the last
in a reverse order of creation
returning what you borrowed
salt & a fresh life
going up the hole
again

everything points to the sadness of the land
first the animals were scoured off
or first the Indians and then the animals
Seneca, Tuscarora, Chippewa, Ojibway
names that clog the tongue still
like trying to eat a peck of salt

the bear, the beaver, the wolf, the eagle
the tree-of-doves disappeared at a crack
virgin forests groaned and lay down
great fires were built to clear the fields
then stumps were pulled like rotten teeth
and rocks were piled on stone-sleds and moved

now, on a rise above Cayuga Lake, the land
soars on a summer day as fast as the clouds above it
there is order and peace and you could say
how rich, how beautiful the land
broken into fields (thin boundary woods between)
cattle, corn, barley, wheat, clover
domesticity that sprawls to the horizon
even the barn manure smells sweet

and the blood of Indian or animal
the green sap spilling of trees is gone
or it lingers like the fog in layers
across the highway   or it sometimes hangs
like a slice of moon above the town
it follows the honking of the geese north
it bubbles in the chirr of the cicada
it hesitates and mourns mechanically in the owl
the blood the sadness pours

it taps our shoulder as we move in the house
leads us to the window to look out
rustles in the fields and in the woods in the fall
there   at the edge of vision never caught
more potent than any of our dead
because more alive and demanding   the land
everything points to the sadness of the land

Leaving The City

written on the back of the seat in front of me
was this message:

I LOVE MILDRED KING
WONDER WHO I AM

here is someone who has flown out of himself
I thought   to a holiday in the city
he's got it into his head that he's a lover
and so he flies over the pools and delicious
pits of thwarted or forbidden love
yet plaintively cries of *wonder who I am*
send shock waves out and they return
who I am in so many unexpected ways
he is amazed   and seeing   for instance
a Murdock Brothers Truck heaped with watermelon
cold green buttocks piled so firm
slippery thumping breasts nodding each on each
with Brother Murdock in control
rolling down the highway   he is moved
to take out his pen and write
a message on the seat in front of him
so full of sentiment that he could cry
at this moment   just for sentiment's sake

there were three epiphanies   three wringers
he called them that washed the city away

he saw two fat blackbirds sitting in a pine tree
like smug shopkeepers in their shop   it was a shock

sweeter yet   he saw a woman
kneeling in the dirt and had visions

of pink peonies   tomatoes   squash
gardens   loaves   and fish
he practically bloomed out

and last   looking down a steep grade
he saw a fresh pebbly stream at the bottom
so clear   meandering   banked in green
his blood came back

it was a headlong and simple birth

what the old frog said

the first stick breaks without bud or blossom
the second stick bends forward stiffly
the third stick is soft as mice and has a bud
the fourth stick swells and sweats with the strain
the fifth stick opens its sweet sky of flowers
the sixth stick waves and plumps in the sun
the seventh stick is vacant and badly snarled
the eighth stick splatters and breathes mud
the ninth stick is sharp as a locust thorn
but the tenth stick's memory is the greenest one